GARLANDS

Natalie Wright

W9-AAC-098

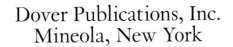

Dover Publications, Inc.
Mineola, New York

Bibliographical Note

Make in a Day: Garlands is a new work,
first published by Dover Publications, Inc., in 2017.

International Standard Book Number

ISBN-13: 978-0-486-81495-7
ISBN-10: 0-486-81495-5

Manufactured in the United States by LSC Commmunications
81495501   2017
www.doverpublications.com

CONTENTS

Vintage Fabric Garland   1

Mini Sewn Paper Banner   4

Felt Leaf Banner   8

Honeycomb Banner   12

Photograph Garland   16

Yarn Garland   20

Piñata Garland   24

Paper Leaf Garland   28

Watercolor Garland   32

Felt Bow Garland   36

Plastic Canvas Garland   40

Fairy Lights Garland   44

Mixed Metallic Banner   48

Paper Fan Banner   52

Crepe Paper Flower Garland   56

Here's a secret: I am a 1970's genetically modified test-tube baby who was bred to be super awesome and creative. Okay, not really, but my father was a home builder, and my mother a crafter and event planner. So naturally I was born to love getting my hands dirty and make pretty things. I am also a lefty. It's very important that everyone knows this, because it means you have an extra dose of creative crafty coolness. For real.

My background is in photography, which is always helpful when you want to make a project that didn't turn out so great look perfect and amazing. I love paper crafting while watching Netflix, throwing parties for vague holidays, and spending time with my four fabulous children at home. Well, except for the last one. She's a bit of a stinker. I have a fun forty-something hipster husband who supports my creative craziness, cooks a paleo lunch for me every day, and vacuums the house every Sunday. Yup, he is a keeper.

In my spare time, I share my creative endeavors on my personal blog, www.natalme.com. I love to work with paint and paper, which you will see a lot of in this book. The inspiration to create it came when I found that I just couldn't throw away any of the garlands and banners I designed for various parties and events. My house is now filled with all of those pretty handmade projects.

To keep an eye on all of my creative adventures (and failures!), be sure to follow me on Instagram at @natalme.

Vintage Fabric Garland

Pinking shears are essential for your craft stash. They are great for beginner sewers who aren't yet ready to navigate high-end serger machines or complicated stitching. Pinking shears cut the fabric at an angle that makes fraying next to impossible. They cut easily through light or heavy weighted fabrics, making them an ideal tool for fun vintage fabrics that you can find in antique and thrift stores.

When looking for vintage fabric, don't just look at fabric cut by the yard. Vintage dish towels and bed linens often have patterns and prints reflective of an older era. If you aren't able to find vintage fabric in your local town, there are some really pretty vintage-inspired prints that can be bought online.

To make the vintage fabric garland, you will need:

* Vintage fabric quilt squares, or ½ yard of vintage fabric

* Pinking shears

* Hot glue gun and glue sticks

* Twine

1 First, cut your fabric into 2½" x 4½" rectangles using your pinking shears. You can use the same fabric for your entire banner, or use lots of vintage-inspired prints like I did!

2 Cut a V-shaped notch in the bottom of your rectangle piece to create a pennant. Repeat with all of your fabric banner pieces.

3 Flip pennant piece over, and adhere twine to each pennant using your hot glue gun.

4 Hang the banner with low-tack adhesive tape. See how it looks in a bedroom or living room, on a mantel, or at a party! You can even hang it up outside if you use an outdoor-safe glue.

TIP: Fabric banners look oh-so-lovely hanging in a window. The colorful semi-transparent fabric allows light to gently shine through, enhancing that whimsical vintage feel.

Mini Sewn Paper Banner

It can be so easy to get intimidated by the sheer number of colors and patterns available for any project. My favorite thing about this garland is that the idea is actually very simple: By taking similar colors and repeating shapes and patterns, you get some serious "wow-factor" out of an idea that's really easy to pull off. What's your favorite color to work with? Choose 4–5 colors along that color scheme, and get cutting! Cut lots of small shapes, and when it's time to sew, repeat colors or patterns in any order you like. Embrace the chaos, and I promise you will love the results.

To make the mini sewn paper banner you will need:

* 12" x 12" solid colored scrapbook paper

* Paper trimmer

* Sewing machine

* Scissors

* Thread

1 Use your scissors and paper trimmer to cut 1" x 12" strips of paper. Cut 5–6 strips from each paper color, depending on how long you want your banners to be.

2 Cut the rectangular shapes 2½" in length. For the triangles, cut 1" squares, then cut in half diagonally. For the circles, you can cut 1" squares into round shapes, or you may wish to use a basic round paper punch instead.

3 Repeat cutting shapes with each colored cardstock so you have 60–80 pieces for the smaller shapes, and 25–35 for the larger ones.

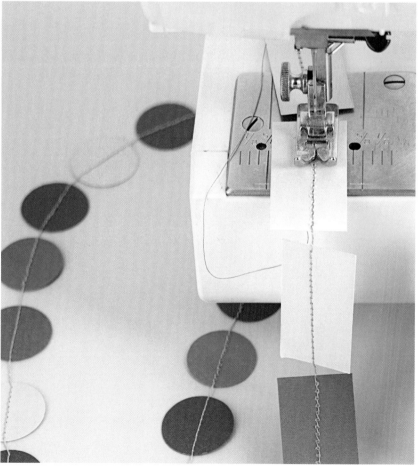

4 Arrange your pieces together with like shapes or colors. Sew each assortment in five pieces, each a foot long.

5 Sew your banner pieces together in your desired pattern.

6 Repeat sewing each strand until you have six or seven long strands of sewn paper.

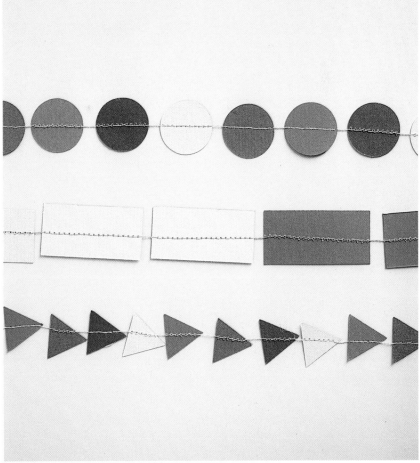

TIP: To keep your banners from tangling, tape them vertically on your wall one at a time, being careful not to cross them over each other.

Felt Leaf Banner

The mantel in my house was begging for attention, but I am a big believer in decorating just once for the entire year. Fireplace mantels can sure be tricky! They are often the centerpiece for holiday décor and embellishments, so it's easy to get carried away with buying and storing holiday décor. They can be difficult to style, too. Some only have a few narrow inches of depth, and they are sooooo long.

Banners and garlands are the perfect solution, and working with nature-inspired green hues make mantel decor look lovely all year 'round. Instead of using paper, go for a more durable material such as fabric or felt. A high-quality wool blend felt will last for years, and can even be gently washed if needed. If holiday decorating is your thing, a felt leaf banner will complement seasonal décor when you feel like putting in that extra touch.

To make the felt leaf banner, you will need:

* Felt sheets in light, medium, and dark green

* Twine

* Hot glue gun and glue sticks

* Scissors

1 Using your scissors and felt sheets, create leaf pieces by folding felt sheets in 3" sections, and cutting felt fabric pieces in a half-oval shape.

2 Continue cutting leaves until you have 75–85 pieces. I used about 80 leaves for my mantel banner; the amount you need will depend on how long you want yours to be.

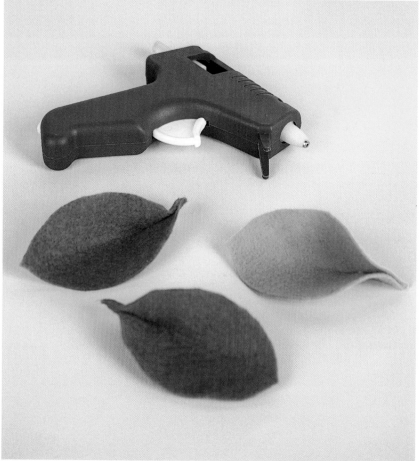

3 Pinch and glue the end of each leaf tip. This will give each leaf added depth and dimension. Allow glue to fully cool.

4 Determine the length of your banner, and cut a piece of twine accordingly. Adhere your felt leaves to the twine using your hot glue gun. Stagger the leaves so they slightly overlap as you go.

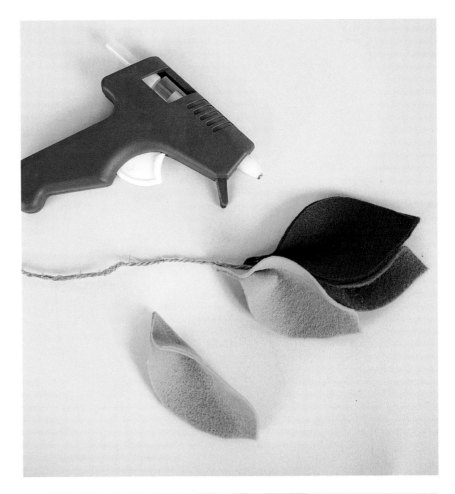

5 Add any additional glue needed on the back of your felt fabric for stability. Allow the glue to fully cool. Then hang the banner, and enjoy! I cut some additional larger leaves to make a coordinating wreath to go above my mantel. I love that it gives my mantel a classic look year 'round.

Honeycomb Banner

There's a hidden secret behind crafting with honeycomb paper: It's not as hard as it looks! More and more craft stores are providing honeycomb sheets pre-made for crafting. All you need are scissors and glue to make your own honeycomb creations! If you are new to crafting with honeycomb paper, start with basic shapes like diamonds and circles. After some practice, you will be ready to cut more intricate shapes like summer-inspired pineapples or Christmas trees. The options with honeycomb paper really are endless!

To make the honeycomb banner, you will need:

* 12" x 12" colored cardstock
* Colored honeycomb paper
* Hot glue gun and glue sticks
* Scissors
* Pencil

1 Using your pencil, draw a 1½" half circle on your honeycomb paper using a lid or circular container as a template. Be sure to trace your pattern on the side of the honeycomb paper that has an adhesive seam, allowing the paper to stay together.

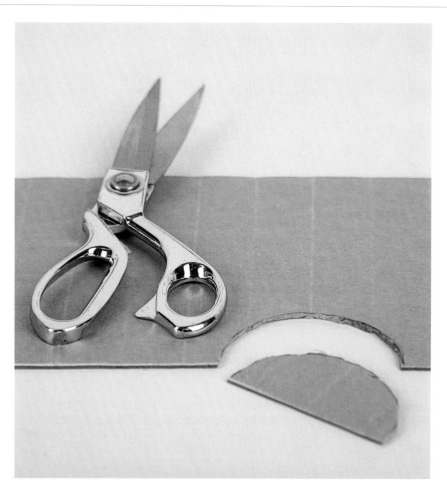

2 Carefully cut out the half circle with your scissors. Honeycomb paper is really thick, so the sharper the scissors, the better! Unfolded, the circle should measure 3" in diameter.

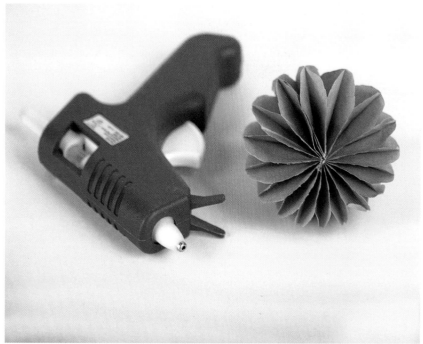

3 Open up and adhere the honeycomb paper in a circle using your hot glue gun and glue sticks. Repeat the process 8–10 times, depending on the desired length of your banner. I cut all my honeycomb balls the same size, but you can change your sizes or colors for variety.

4 Draw and cut out candy wrapper shapes from your colored cardstock. It helps to sketch and cut out a template so you know exactly how you want the finished project to look.

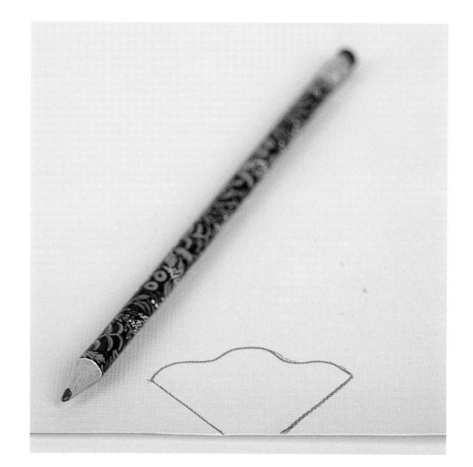

5 Adhere your cut wrapper pieces to each side of the honeycomb paper. Then measure the desired length of your banner, and cut a piece of twine accordingly. Open up and adhere the honeycomb balls around your cut twine. If you want to place them on a flat wall, open only halfway and attach to a 3" paper circle. Hang on your wall for some fabulous customized party décor, and enjoy!

TIP: You can use leftover honeycomb paper scraps to create additional décor for your party. Cupcake toppers and goodie bags look adorable with itty-bitty honeycomb paper balls!

Photograph Garland

I was a photographer long before I was ever a crafter. I am a big believer in documenting our daily lives, and taking pictures of my family helps me preserve those cherished memories. I take pictures when we travel, but the simple mundane things we do at home are often my favorite to capture. I shoot often, so showcasing all of our photos is just an impossible task. Early on I decided to rotate my favorite photos, and this garland makes it easy to change pictures on a monthly or weekly basis. It's also easy to accommodate whatever size or orientation you like to print your photos. The binder clips are easy to slide back and forth, allowing for more or less room in between each of your favorite memories.

To make the photograph garland, you will need:

* Pompom ribbon
  in pink and white

* Black & white binder clips

* Fujifilm Instax®
  or Polaroid ZIP® Printer

* Photo paper

* Scissors

1. Use a mini photo printer to print your favorite photos. Don't have a mini photo printer? Download a free Instax photo template to make your own printable photos at natalme.com/ free-instax-mini-photoshop-template.

2. Cut a 30" section of white pompom ribbon. The length of your photograph garland will really depend on how many photos you want to hang, so be sure to adjust your project accordingly.

3 Cut the pink pompom ribbon into 3" pieces. The quantity will depend on how many binder clips you want to use. I would suggest 9–10 pieces.

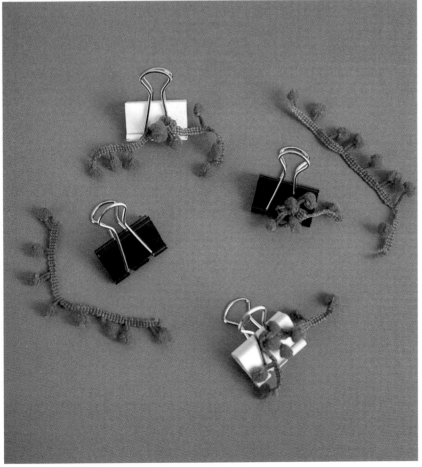

4 Tie the pink pompom pieces onto the front of each binder clip.

5 String your black and white binder clips onto your white pompom ribbon, spacing them about 1–2" apart. Be sure to clip them on in an alternating manner, going from black to white.

6 Add photos onto your binder clips. If you are hanging these on a wall, clip a single photo. If you hang them in an open area, clip photos back to back so you can enjoy both sides of the banner. Hang your banner with a low-tack adhesive or brad nails. Switch out your photos whenever you like!

Yarn Garland

Yarn is one of my favorite craft supplies to work with. It's strong enough to hold a bundle of twigs together, it's a great substitute for ribbon on a package or gift bag, it's easy to dye any color you like, and it's very inexpensive to buy. There are so many great options now with the weight, color, and material blend as well!

My favorite thing about this project is that even though I used some darker colors, the sunlight from my windows still shines through the yarn threads each morning. And the entire project costs just a few dollars to make! If you have little helpers at home, this is a great project to try with your children or grandchildren. My daughter and I worked together on ours, and we were able to finish the project in just two hours. Not bad for a home décor project that she will be able to enjoy for a really long time!

To make the yarn garland, you will need:

* Yarn skeins in 4–5 colors

* Sharp scissors

* Pompom maker (if desired)

1 Cut forty 24" strands of each yarn color for each banner section. I used four different colors of yarn for my long-hanging pieces.

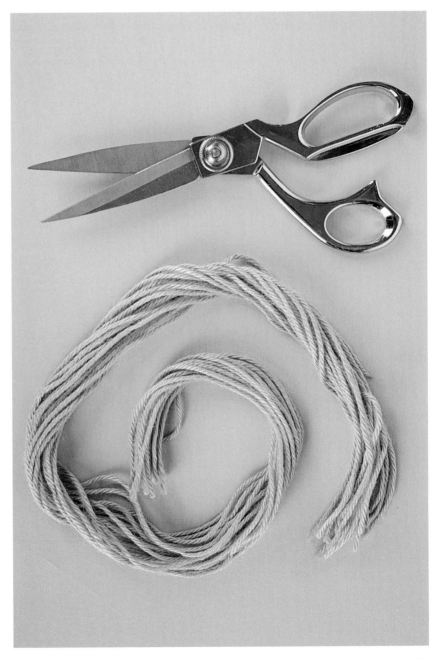

2 Cut a 3' section of yarn to be your main piece that you will knot everything on. Knot it at each end to prevent fraying. Start looping your yarn one strand at a time, by first laying down a single strand of yarn folded in half. At the top of the fold, lay the loop underneath your main piece.

3 Loop the end pieces of your strand through the loop, pulling tight. Repeat the process, working from left to right.

4 Continue looping your yarn pieces until you have tightly woven about forty pieces of one color in a row. Add a yarn pompom if desired, then repeat with the next color.

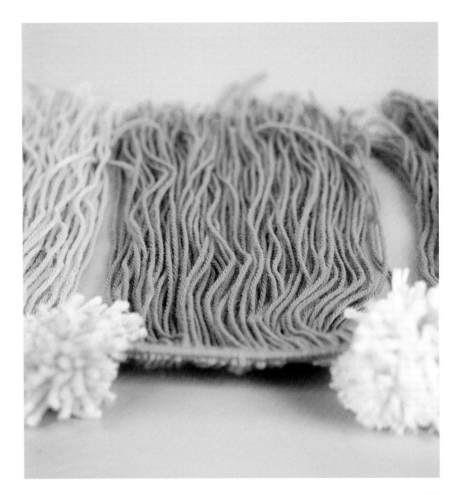

5 When you are finished with looping on your pieces, trim each yarn section at an angle, creating a pennant-like shape. Then hang up your banner and enjoy!

Piñata Garland

I was born on Cinco de Mayo, and I can't remember a birthday growing up where I didn't have a piñata to smash open! A few years ago I realized a large-scale piñata always made for a huge mess in my backyard, and inevitably someone felt left out from not getting to be the one to smash it open, or not getting enough candy in the chaos. I decided to try something new last year: mini-piñatas for all the party guests! By why not accomplish two tasks in one? Use the itty-bitty piñatas as decoration, then allow the guests to each smash their own at the end of the party. My mini piñata banner was born!

If you don't want to ruin your handmade décor, mini piñatas also make great party favor boxes. Tip: Pre-fill your piñatas before you embellish them. Be careful not to fill them too much! The more candy you use, the more weight they pull down on your garland.

To make the piñata garland, you will need:

* 12" x 12" colored cardstock in 5–7 colors

* Paper trimmer

* Fringe scissors

* 4" x 4" x 4" square gift boxes

* Permanent adhesive runner

* White ribbon

1 Trim colored cardstock down to 1½" x 12" pieces. You will need 8–10 strips of paper for each piñata.

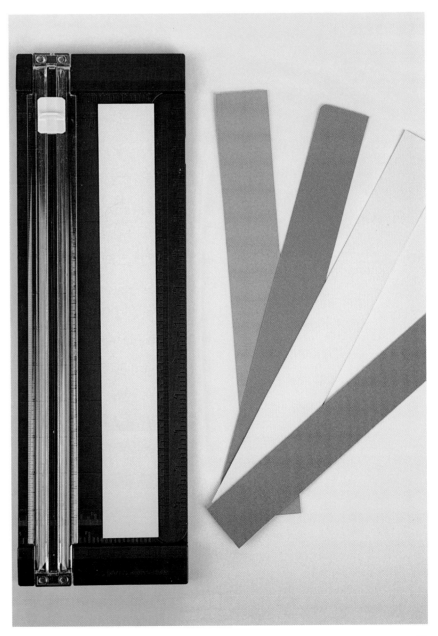

2 Use your fringe scissors to shred each paper strip, cutting it ¾ of the way up. Attach each strip to the gift box with your adhesive runner, alternating colored cardstock.

3 Continue to attach the fringe, working from the bottom to the top of each gift box.

4 Repeat steps until you have enough mini piñatas to create a garland.

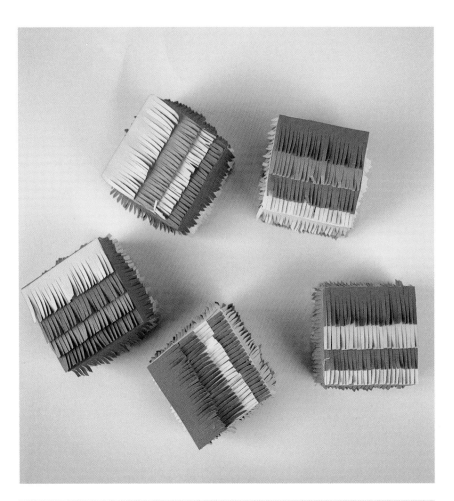

5 Adhere white ribbon to the top of each piñata. String the piñata boxes together to create a party garland.

Paper Leaf Garland

Spring is my absolute favorite season. The promise of warmth, sunshine, and growth outside makes my heart so happy after a long, snow-filled season. I find that I craft the most in the spring. I cut the most blooms from my yard, and it's my favorite time to get my hands dirty in the garden. I love seeing the buds on trees and the beginning sprouts of leaves, so it just naturally makes sense that I'm drawn to re-creating it indoors. This itty-bitty paper leaf garland is a subtle reminder of spring, and I love how it looks in my house year 'round. Of all of the paper craft projects in my home, it gets the most compliments, and I have helped many friends re-create their own pretty paper version.

To make the paper leaf garland, you will need:

* Green cardstock in four different shades
* Stick or twig measuring 12–18"
* Liquid glue
* Twine
* Scissors
* Pencil

1. Draw a 1" leaf pattern on the green cardstock, creating a leaf template.

2. Trace and cut out multiple paper leaves from each green-colored cardstock.

3 Your leaves should vary slightly in color and size. The amount of leaves needed for this project depends on how wide and long you want your leaf garland to be. I used around 85–100 leaves for each of my single strands. This is definitely a "labor of love"-type of project. Just keep cutting!

4 After cutting your leaf shapes, fold each leaf in half, creasing the seam. This will give your leaves some added dimension when you are ready to adhere them together.

5 Cut three 4½' sections of twine, and two 4' pieces. Using your twine and paper adhesive, adhere the paper leaves carefully, staggering them side to side for added dimension.

6 Continue adhering paper leaves until you have five strands of leaves, two slightly shorter than the rest.

7 Attach your twine strands to the top of your twig. Add another section of twine at either end for hanging.

Watercolor Garland

Working with watercolor paint is a great way to expand your artistic talents. Even the simplest circle can naturally replicate a lovely painting. The dried cake-like paints are incredibly malleable with just a little water, but at the same time very unforgiving if you don't know how to use them correctly. I always suggest that watercolors be approached in layers. The first time I made this banner, it was way too soft and dull. By adding additional layers of color, I achieved some really fun variations of blues and reds. Practice first on some scrap paper, and remember to embrace the imperfections!

To make the watercolor garland, you will need:

* Watercolor paints
* Watercolor paper
* Paintbrush
* Adhesive tape runner

* White craft glue
* Pencil
* String or twine
* Scissors

1 Use a round plastic lid or container to trace circles onto your white watercolor paper. My circles are about 6" in diameter.

2 Carefully cut out each paper circle. Watercolor paper comes in different paper weights, so I would suggest using a heavy, thick paper and sharp scissors to help you cut each shape.

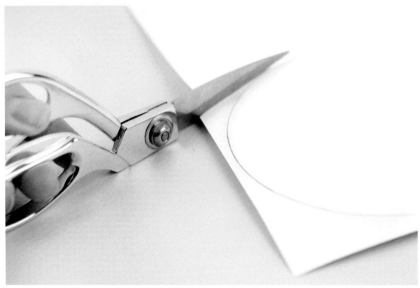

3 Repeat several times, depending on your desired banner length. I cut about 18 circles for mine.

4 Using your paintbrush and water, paint watercolor paper circles in a back-and-forth direction.

TIP: You can also use acrylic craft paint by adding 3 parts water to 1 part paint.

5 Paint all of your circles using as much or as little paint as you like. Allow them to dry completely.

6 Adhere string or twine to the backs of your circles, spacing them 1–2" apart. Then hang your banner up for display! Watercolor paper has a really nice texture, so it makes for a lovely party backdrop. Get creative with your watercolor paints. Splattering, dipping, and blending are all great ways to manipulate watercolor paints on paper.

Felt Bow Garland

If you can tie a single knot, I promise you can pull off this garland! Simple strips of fabric make the perfect foundation for a knot garland, and this project is a great solution for leftover fabric scraps. I suggest felt for this project, as it tends to have a heavier weight. Inexpensive felt sheets are a great material, but heavy weighted wool felt will work beautifully, too. The denser the fabric, the stiffer your knots will be. Choose the material based on how you want the end result to look. You can always use a cotton blend fabric as well—just add a few extra fabric scraps to each bow.

This banner is a favorite to make with friends. Craft nights are really about the social interaction, right? I always love a project that takes just a few minutes to make, and friends can make it as simple or complicated as they like!

To make the felt bow garland, you will need:

- 8½" x 11" felt sheets in mint, peach, and off-white
- Rotary cutter
- Twine
- Scissors

1. Using your rotary cutter, cut long strips of felt fabric measuring ¾" wide x 8½" long. Cut six strips out of each felt piece.

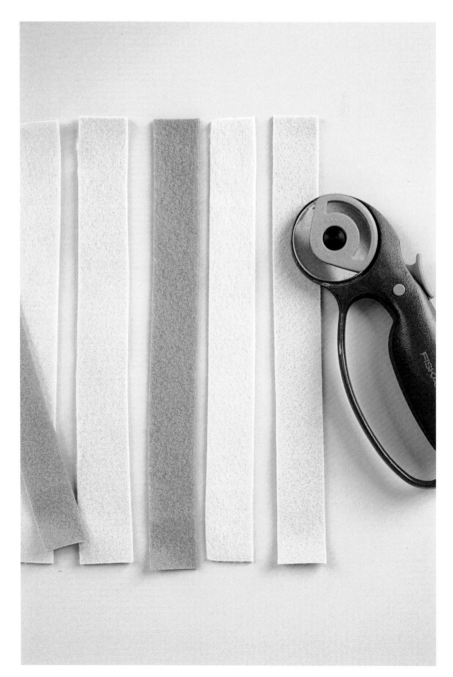

TIP: Be sure to use a rotary cutter mat so you don't ruin your tabletop surface. If you don't have a rotary cutter, just carefully cut long strips with your scissors.

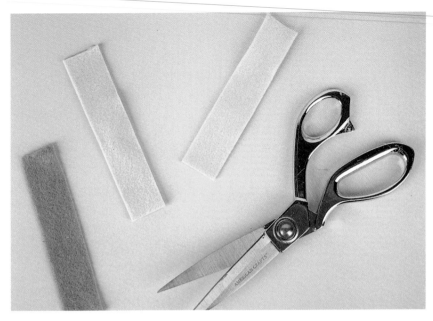

2 Fold strips in half, and cut on fold. You should now have a dozen pieces measuring ¾" x 4¼" in each color.

3 Measure 1½" yards of twine. Lay the twine down, and tie your felt pieces on one at a time with a single knot.

4 Each knot bow should have three pieces of felt, one of each color.

5 Repeat until you have over a dozen felt bows tied to your twine. Slide bows around so they are spaced evenly. Then hang the banner with a low-tack adhesive. The fun thing about this project is the felt knot bows are really quick and easy to make, so you can make the garland as long or short as you like! The quality of your fabric will also determine how stiff or soft your bows are.

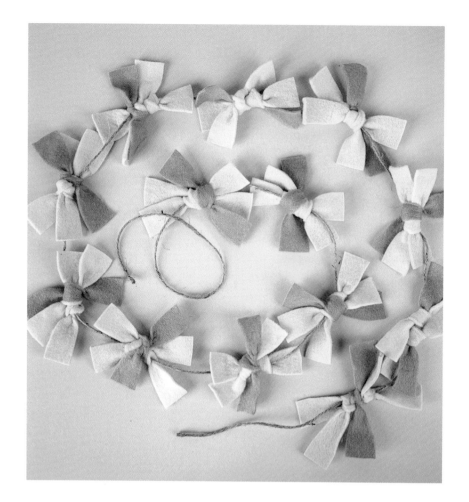

Plastic Canvas Garland

Remember cutting up plastic canvas as a kid? Stitching little tissue-box houses and Christmas ornaments was a big part of the time I spent with my grandmother. I loved how easy it was to construct a box, and I was always surprised that yarn held it together! Now my kids love crafting with plastic canvas. It's a very durable material, and it's a great tool for working on fine motor skills. It's inexpensive, too!

My favorite thing about this banner is that it's very outdoor-friendly. The plastic material holds up beautifully, and you can even use a heavy weighted yarn, ribbon, or twine for this project. Because it weighs more than a fabric banner, it's less likely to be disturbed by wind and outdoor elements. I also love that you need just a few supplies to make it. It's a win-win when I want to make some fun décor for an indoor or outdoor party!

To make the plastic canvas garland, you will need:

* Large, colorful poster board in various colors

* Long wooden dowel

* Bulky weight yarn in various colors

* Scissors

* Large pompom maker

* Adhesive boat decal letters (can be purchased at any home improvement store)

* Hot glue gun and glue sticks

* Optional: colored ribbon

1 Using your scissors and ruler, measure and cut your plastic canvases down to 4" x 5½" pieces. You will be able to get eight pieces from two 8½" x 11" pieces of plastic canvas.

2 Cut a V shape from the bottom of each rectangle, creating a pennant shape.

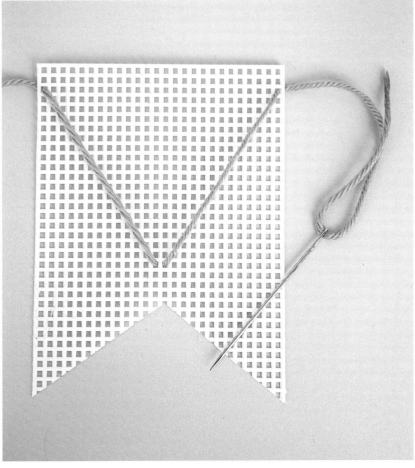

3 Choose your first color of yarn, and stitch a V shape onto the pennant pieces, linking them together. Continue linking plastic canvas pieces together to create desired length, then knot at end.

4 Repeat with your second and third yarn colors, slightly staggering the height on each pennant piece.

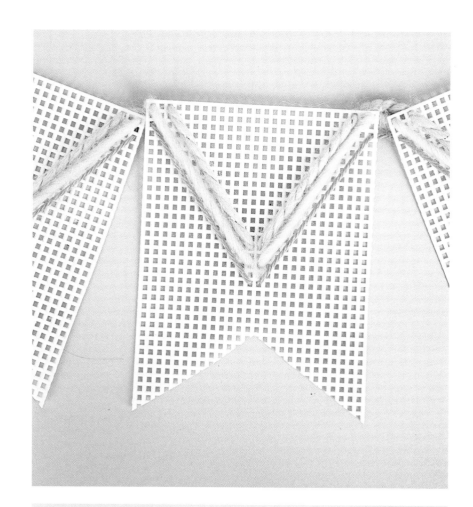

5 Continue stitching your plastic canvas until your pattern covers the entire piece. Keep your project simple with a single design, or alternate patterns depending on the look you want.

Fairy Lights Garland

This project incorporates some of my current favorite craft supplies: ink sprays and itty-bitty fairy lights! These lovely little copper light strands come in all shapes and sizes, and the included battery packs make this banner easy to use indoors or out. Try to find a light strand with copper wiring. It's easy to bend and shape, and can be adhered to paper with low-temp glue gun sticks.

If you haven't tried out ink spritzers yet, you are missing out! They are renowned by mixed media artists, but can be used in simple paper crafting, too. Because they intentionally spray all over the place, they are a good reminder to embrace the imperfections in your projects. Ink spritzers are also ideal for blending colors, and often come in formulas that have iridescent materials that reflect light.

To make the fairy lights garland, you will need:

* Watercolor paper
* Ink spritzers
* Fairy light strand
* Twine
* Low-temp hot glue gun and glue sticks
* Pencil
* Scissors

1 Create a triangle pattern measuring 3" wide by 4½" tall. Cut and use as a template.

2 Trace and cut 8–10 pieces, depending on the length of your fairy lights.

3 In a protected area, spritz your pennant pieces with ink spritzers. The more you spray, the darker the color will be.

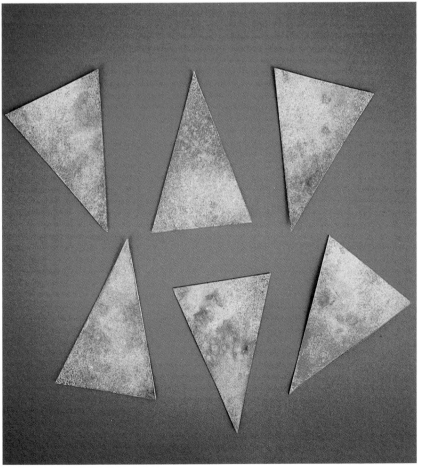

4 Apply your ink in a varied pattern for a fun watercolor look! Allow pennants to fully dry before finishing your project.

5 Using your low-temp hot glue gun, carefully adhere the backs of the pennant pieces to your fairy lights, making sure you adhere them on the copper wire, in between the tiny lights.

TIP: Be sure to use a low-temp glue gun and glue sticks so you don't damage your light strand.

6 Allow the glue to fully cool before hanging the banner on your wall. Add small pieces of tape to the back if you feel like the hot glue isn't offering enough stability. Hide the battery pack behind one of the pennant pieces, allowing easy access to the on/off switch.

Mixed Metallic Banner

Paper printing technology has allowed more and more manufacturers to create incredible metallic sheens and colors on paper. The result: From matte to high luster, there are a lot of fabulous options for paper crafters. And when you can get one metallic color, why not get them all, right? This multi-colored metallic banner looks great in both natural and indoor lighting. It adds that extra touch of sparkle that we always want when planning an upscale party or soirée.

From summer celebrations to New Year's Eve, metallic paper is always a great tool to have on hand in your craft stash. To find metallic paper, try the scrapbook paper section at your local crafts store. For larger-scale projects, metallic poster board gives you a large sheet of heavy-weight paper for just a few dollars.

To make the mixed metallic banner, you will need:

* Colored metallic cardstock in 4–5 different hues

* Hot glue gun and glue sticks

* Scissors

* Pencil

* Gold thread or twine

1. Draw a single 1½" circle and cut it out to use as a template. Use a container lid or cap to help if needed.

2 Use your circle template to trace and cut 12–15 metallic circles from each metallic-colored paper.

3 Adhere circles in a repetitive pattern onto your gold twine with your hot glue gun. Space them about ½" apart as you go.

4 Each banner will need around 15–20 circles, depending on how long you want it to be. Try making one that is really long, or several shorter versions like I did, and string them together to cover more vertical wall space.

5 After creating your metallic banners, hang them on your wall using a low-tack adhesive tape. I layered three together for my party tablescape, but you can cover as much wall space as you like. Be sure to have good lighting in your space so the banner really shines!

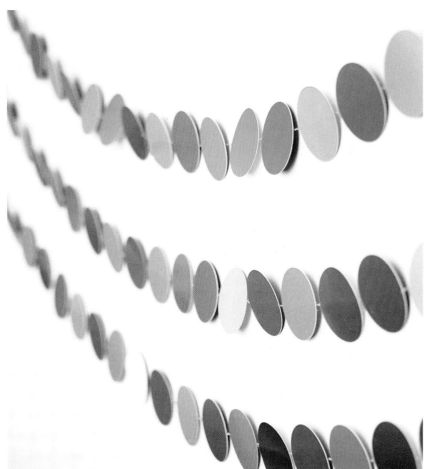

Paper Fan Banner

Did you know that in Japan, paper fans date all the way back to the sixth century? They were created for social and court activities, and often featured detailed paintings and embellishments. Today, crafters have found that paper fans give much depth and texture to their projects. Because each fan can be made in a matter of minutes, they can be used for a quick and easy party decoration. From inexpensive copy paper to luxurious Japanese rice paper, fans will always be one of my favorite go-to projects when I want to create a lot of "wow-factor" with only a little bit of time.

To make the paper fan banner, you will need:

* 12" x 12" cardstock in black, gray, and white

* Trim and score board, or 12" ruler

* Bone folder tool (optional)

* Hot glue gun and glue sticks

* Scissors

* Twine

1 Cut your paper down to 6" x 12". Using your trim and score board, or a ruler and embossing tool, emboss a straight line on your paper at 1" intervals.

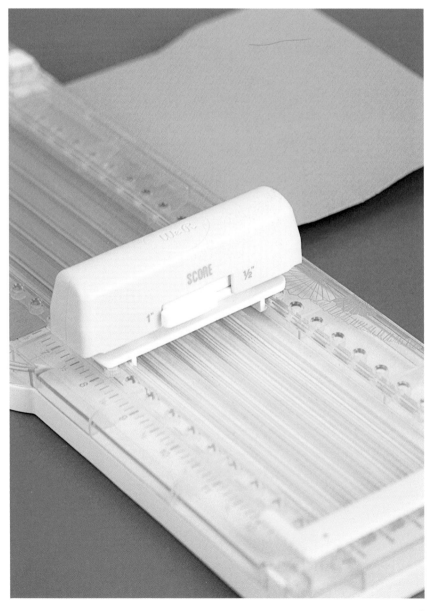

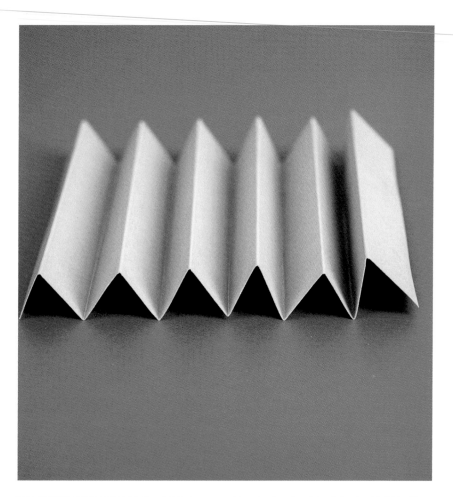

2 Accordion fold your scored paper, creating a paper fan. Use a bone folder tool if you need help creasing the paper evenly.

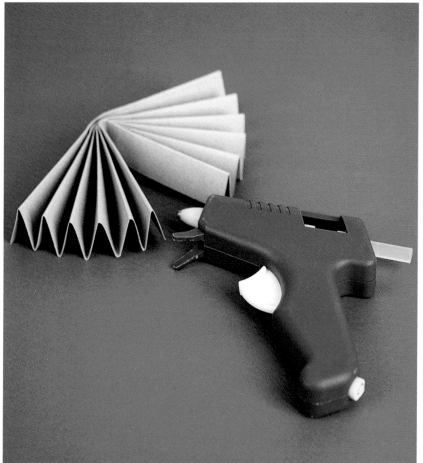

3 Using your hot glue gun, fold your accordion paper in half, and glue the center together.

4 Repeat making paper fans with the remaining cardstock paper. Adhere your fans together, creating a long fan banner, gluing them right side up, upside down; and repeating the pattern.

5 Continue gluing the paper fans together until you have your desired length. My banner is about four feet wide, but you can make yours as long or as short as you'd like. Hang on your walls for a party or as home décor with low-tack tape.

Crepe Paper Flower Garland

My youngest daughter has been begging for a desk in her room, and I knew that she was seeking something that would function for both work and play. Homework is just a part of life at our house, and my kids also love having creative time. So I wanted to make a simple space for her that inspired her to work hard and have fun, too! She loves being outside and planting flowers with me, so paper flowers were a natural fit. Since she wanted to help, I turned to crepe paper. It's an inexpensive material that's easy to cut, shape, and glue together. Because it's so easy to pinch and twist, it's a very forgiving paper that is perfect for small hands to work with. Each bloom takes just a few minutes to make, and don't be afraid to let little ones help you! You will be surprised at how easy these blooms are to make together.

* Crepe paper in green, pink, and orange

* Pompom ribbon

* Hot glue gun and glue sticks

* Scissors

1 Using your scissors, cut oval petal shapes out of orange, green, and pink crepe paper each measuring between 2" and 3" long.

2 For each flower, you will need two green leaves and twelve pink or orange petals.

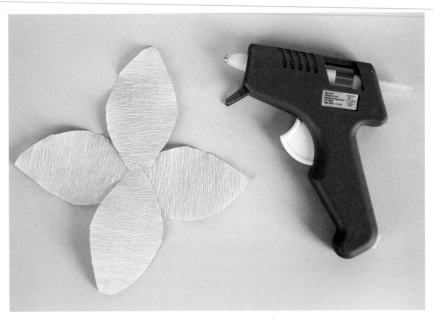

3 Using your hot glue gun, adhere four petals together at the base.

4 Layer four more petals with glue, then an additional four on top with your hot glue gun. Be sure to stagger each layer.

5 While the hot glue is still warm, flip over your petals and pinch the back center of the flower. This will give your flower some extra depth and dimension. You can always add an extra dab of hot glue to warm it up again, or to hold it in place.

6 Adhere two green leaves to the back of your flower. Repeat the process, creating eight finished flowers.

7 Adhere pompom ribbon to the back of your flower garland, and hang it on your wall with low-tack tape.